Harmonica for Kids

How to Play, Master the Basics, and Blow the Blues Away

Table of Contents

Introduction

Do you want to pick up a new instrument, but you're not sure what to get? A harmonica is the perfect choice! It's small and easy to use, although you'll need to learn how to play it right. Harmonicas can make beautiful music when in the hands of a master. While you won't be playing like John Popper or Bob Dylan right out of the gate, with enough practice and a desire to improve, you'll be on your way to joining their ranks as an expert harmonica player. The only thing you have to bring with you is a harmonica and a positive attitude.

If this is your first time picking up a harmonica, this book will guide you every step of the way. From how to hold it to where you place your lips, what techniques you need to use to play notes, and even how to play some simple songs, this book is a one-stop shop for everything you need to know to get started. It always seems overwhelming to begin a new hobby, but the key is to take it one step at a time. Don't look at the top of the mountain—just focus on the path right in front of you. Before you know it, you'll have climbed to the summit and learned all about how to play the harmonica.

This book isn't just a how-to guide—it'll be your constant companion along your journey. You can refer back to it whenever you need a reminder about something or want to refresh your skills. As you improve, you'll get the chance to try out more difficult techniques that will push your abilities to the next level. By the time you're done, you'll have all the tools you need to start advancing from beginner to expert. The only thing that can stop you is yourself. As long as you believe you have what it takes to become a great harmonica player, you'll be able to achieve your dream!

Chapter 1: Introduction to Harmonicas

Some of the best harmonica players out there like to say that the harmonica is easy to play but hard to master. It looks pretty simple. All you have to do to make it play is to blow on it. Go ahead and give it a try. You're going to get a nice sound no matter where you blow on a harmonica. That's the easy part. But playing actual music? That's where it gets a bit tricky. Before we get to the harder stuff, you should know more about the instrument itself.

It's always helpful to know all about how something is made and how it works before you start using it. If you've ever gotten a toy that you had to put together, you know that it comes with instructions. You follow the instructions to get all the pieces in the right place, and then you understand how it's supposed to work. This is just like that, except the harmonica is already built when you get it. But when you finish learning about how a harmonica is put together, you'll have a better understanding of how it makes music when you play it.

Harmonica Overview

Harmonicas are known by a few other names around the world: mouth organ, mouth harp, and French harp. It's a popular instrument in music like the blues, jazz, rock, country, folk, and classical. You play the harmonica mainly with your mouth, but you can use your hands to add flourishes to the sound. To know more about it, we'll go over how it produces that sound when you blow into the harmonica, including each of the major pieces that make up the instrument.

What Is a Wind Instrument?

Wind instruments, sometimes classified as aerophones, are instruments that need air to pass through them in order to be played. The harmonica is considered a free-reed wind instrument. This means that it has something called a "resonator" that vibrates when air enters it. These vibrations cause a sound to be made, and the actual pitch of the sound is determined by how fast the resonator vibrates. Wind instruments include a wide range of different classes of musical instruments, such as the following:

- Woodwind Instruments: Saxophones, clarinets, oboes, flutes, bassoons, bagpipes, ocarinas, and recorders.
- Brass Instruments: Trumpets, trombones, horns, tubas, olifants, and euphoniums.
- Reedless Instruments: Didgeridoos, calliopes, pyrophones, boomwhackers, pan flutes, and bullroarers.

- Free Reed Instruments: Harmonicas, pitch pipes, accordions, concertinas, melodicas, and reed organs.

Parts of a Harmonica

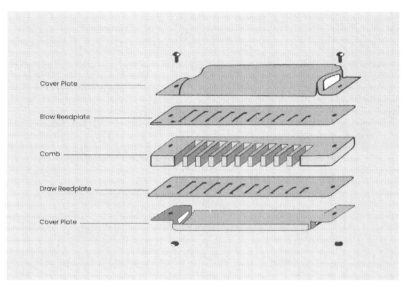

A harmonica is made up of 5 main parts: the comb, reed plate, cover plates, wind savers, and mouthpiece. Each piece has its own job when it comes to making a harmonica play. Although you probably won't ever have to assemble or reassemble your harmonica by yourself, it's helpful to have an idea about what their purpose is in the operation of the instrument. Here is a list of the parts of a harmonica and what each one does:

Comb

The comb makes up the main body of a harmonica. When the instrument is taken apart, it looks like a hair comb, which is where it got its name. While harmonica combs were originally made out of wood, they can now be made from both plastic and metal as well. They form air chambers for the reed when put together with the reed plates. If you're looking at a fully assembled harmonica, the comb is the part in the middle with all the little square chambers.

Reed Plates

There are 2 reed plates that sit on top and bottom of the comb. They're usually made out of metal, especially brass, but they can also be made of steel or aluminum. Some reed plates on cheaper harmonicas might be made from plastic instead. The reeds themselves are attached to both sides of the reed plate, but they have different jobs. The reeds on the side that touch the comb make sound when you blow into the mouthpiece, while those on the opposite side make sound when you use suction by inhaling.

Cover Plates

The cover plates are the outer shell of the harmonica, going on top of the reed plates. They're generally made of metal, but as with most parts of the instrument, they can also come in wood or plastic. Two varieties of cover plates exist: the open design is intended to be held while playing; and enclosed design, which lets you play louder and has a richer tone. Any harmonica that includes special additions, like a bell that can be rung with a button, is usually attached to the cover plates.

Wind Savers

Wind savers are one-way valves in the chambers created by the comb and reed plates that prevent extra air from leaking out when the harmonica is being played. The wind savers are used when two reeds share a single chamber. If you're playing a draw note by breathing in, the wind-saver valve on the side meant for the blow notes will be sucked close. To hold them in place, they can be manufactured from thin plastic, leather, knit paper, or Teflon strips that are bonded to the reed plates. Wind savers are typically found in harmonicas that are chromatic, chord, or octave-tuned.

Mouthpiece

The mouthpiece is the part of the harmonica that you put your lips on in order to play. It can be part of the comb or cover plates, or it can be a separate piece that needs to be attached to the instrument with screws. As with the other parts of the harmonica, they can be made from metal, plastic, or sanded wood. Most mouthpieces are designed to feel comfortable when you're playing, and there are a variety of options, giving you plenty of choices when trying to find one that's the right fit for you. However, slider-based chromatic harmonicas must have a special groove in them for the slide, making the design more uniform across different versions.

Types of Harmonicas

Harmonicas come in a variety of types. Each one has their own unique traits that make them good for different uses. Some harmonicas are better for certain genres of music, and others are made for a specific function, like playing with a group or having a distinct sound. The main types of harmonicas you'll have to choose from include:

Diatonic

Diatonic harmonicas are the most basic type of harmonicas. They're designed to only play a single key. Each hole will give you one note while blowing and another note while drawing. Diatonic harmonicas can only play major notes naturally, although it's possible with techniques like bending to achieve minor notes. Here's a diagram showing the blow and draw notes for a diatonic harmonica tuned to the key of G:

	1	2	3	4	5	6	7	8	9	10
Blow	G	B	D	G	B	D	G	B	D	G
Draw	A	D	F♯	A	C	E	F♯	A	C	E

Chromatic

Chromatic harmonicas use a sliding bar that's activated by a button to redirect the air from the holes in the mouthpiece to one reed plate or the other. Besides buttons, the sliding bar can also be shifted by a lever or a modification on the mouthpiece that lets you do it with your lips, making it hands-free. This function allows you to play additional notes than the ones available with diatonic harmonicas. Most chromatic harmonicas will have a single scale when the sliding bar is inactive, making it play like a diatonic harmonica, and then when the sliding bar is activated, each hole will play a note that's a single semitone higher. Chromatic harmonicas can come in varieties with 10 holes, 12 holes, 14 holes, or 16 holes, expanding the amount of notes that can be played.

Tremolo

Tremolo harmonicas, also called tremolo-tuned harmonicas, are a version of diatonic harmonicas that have two different reeds for each note. The reeds are tuned so that one is slightly sharp and the other is slightly flat. By having two reeds with varying pitches, playing them together gives the harmonica a warbling sound. When the pitches of the two reeds are further apart, the warbling effect is faster, which is considered a "wet" tremolo. If the pitches are closer together, the warbling is slower and called a "dry" tremolo.

Orchestral

Orchestral harmonicas are made for the purpose of being played as part of a group or ensemble. They have a more complicated set of tunings available that use various keys and pitches to go with whatever key the orchestral composition was written in. This way, the harmonicas will remain in tune with the rest of the musicians as they play their songs. There are two types of orchestral harmonicas: melody and chord.

- Melody: The main trait of a melody harmonica is that they have one large comb with only blow reeds on both the top and bottom. Some have a layout that makes it like a piano, where the natural notes are on the bottom reed plate, and the sharps and flats are on the top reed plate.
- Chord: The ability to play up to 48 different chords, including major, minor, seventh, augmented, and diminished chords, is the primary characteristic of a chord harmonica. This type of orchestral harmonica is laid out to have clusters of four notes each. The chord harmonica achieves this by having two reeds in each hole, allowing you to play one chord when you inhale and another when you exhale.

Octave

Octave harmonicas, also called octave-tuned harmonicas, are similar to tremolo harmonicas in how their reeds are laid out and their musical capabilities. The difference is that while tremolo harmonicas have their two reeds in each hole tuned to the same note, only slightly sharp or flat, octave harmonicas have their two reeds tuned to be one octave apart. This results in a stronger, richer sound that doesn't have the warbling effect. If you've ever seen a 12-string guitar, octave harmonicas work on a similar principle.

ChengGong

ChengGong harmonicas are considered a form of diatonic harmonicas, but they have a sliding mouthpiece. They also have 24 holes instead of 10, giving them a wider range of musical notes. The standard ChengGong harmonica plays 3 octaves, going from B2 to D6. Since it has so many notes to choose from, as well as a sliding mouthpiece to shift the pitch of these notes, it can play chords like triads, sixths, sevenths, and ninths, giving them a total of 24 chords to choose from. It's also possible to only play single notes. The main difference between them and traditional diatonic harmonicas is that with ChengGong harmonicas, you can only get blow notes instead of both blow and draw notes.

Pitch Pipe

Pitch pipes are specialty harmonicas that serve as a way to help singers and musicians with other instruments find the right pitch. They are kind of like tuning forks, except instead of needing a whole set in order to cover every possible pitch, it can all be done with a single instrument. Pitch pipes that are chromatic cover the whole range of a 12-note octave and are commonly utilized by choirs and vocalists to assist them match the right note. When used for string instruments like guitars and violins, the pitches are meant to match the notes played on open strings.

Reasons to Play the Harmonica

It's never a bad idea to take up a musical instrument. Learning how to play music has many benefits. As an instrument, the harmonica is a great choice if you're short on space since it's one of the smallest instruments you can play. While there is extra gear you can get, the basic investment is just the harmonica, which can easily fit in your pocket. Some other reasons to play the harmonica include the fact that you can:

- Build confidence
- Reduce stress
- Improve memory
- Express of creativity
- Develop patience
- Sense of accomplishment
- Train coordination
- Become more social

Chapter 2: Getting Started with the Harmonica

Now that you're familiar with the parts of the harmonica and how they work, it's time to actually get everything together so you can learn to play. You will need to buy a harmonica and any extra equipment or accessories to help you play. There are plenty of things you should consider before picking a harmonica to buy. In the beginning, you don't need to spend too much money on gear, but as you become more experienced, you can start adding to your setup. The main thing you should focus on right now is making an informed decision about what type of harmonica to get.

Choosing the Right Harmonica

Picking the right harmonica depends on you
Source: https://www.stockvault.net/photo/141170/utils/inffast#

Finding the right harmonica for yourself mostly comes down to a matter of taste. Think about what you want to use your harmonica for, as in what style of music you want to play, and whether you want to play alone or as part of a group. When it comes time to go out and buy your first harmonica, take the following tips into consideration. They can help you make the right choice and not waste time or money on the wrong type of instrument.

Buy New Instead of Used

It's best to buy your harmonica brand new. This is an instrument you play with your mouth, and the mouthpiece isn't replaceable. Buying a used harmonica means it's already been played by someone else, so besides the fact that you can't be sure it will work right, the bigger concern is about it being covered in germs and bacteria from another person. Luckily, most harmonicas aren't too expensive to buy, so you should be able to afford one that's never been played before.

Pick Your Music Style

The style of music you want to play will change which type of harmonica you should buy. Different musical genres go better with certain types of harmonicas, although it's possible to make any type fit if you are determined to play a specific harmonica. Here are the musical styles that work best with the three most common types of harmonicas:

- Diatonic: Country, blues, rock, soul, and Gospel music
- Chromatic: Jazz and classical music
- Tremolo: Folk music

Getting the Right Key

Most harmonicas that you'll be looking to buy will be tuned to a specific key. Harmonicas in the key of C are the standard for beginners since C is a common key for many songs. There are harmonicas tuned to just about every possible key, and as you get more experience playing the instrument, you might want to buy additional harmonicas in other keys. A dedicated harmonica player will have harmonicas for every key they use when playing music.

Playing Solo or with a Group

Depending on if you intend to play alone or with a group, you might need to choose a different type of harmonica. Diatonic harmonicas are good for playing most music in a certain key, but they are limited in the kinds of things they can do with their sound. Chromatic harmonicas will give you more options for improvising with a group, especially a jazz band. When playing alone, diatonic harmonicas will offer the basic notes you need, but it won't sound as full as a chromatic or orchestral harmonica. Orchestral harmonicas are needed when playing with a large group like an orchestra.

Choose the Best Materials

When you buy your new harmonica, you need to make some decisions about what materials you want them to be made from. The two parts of the instrument that will affect this the most are the comb and the cover plates. You can generally find harmonicas made from whatever combination of materials you want, but keep in mind that this will change how much you have to pay for them. Spending more money on quality materials will give you a longer-lasting instrument with a better sound. Here are some of the options to choose from when picking out your materials:

Comb

The type of material used for the comb of the harmonica will have an effect on how it sounds and plays. It will also affect the price of the instrument since some materials are more expensive to manufacture than others. The three basic types of materials used for harmonica combs include:

- Metal: Combs made from metal usually use stainless steel or aluminum, and tend to be the most expensive option. Metal combs might have a "tinny" sound when played, but for some styles of music, that's a benefit. While it won't get worn down in the same way as other materials, it can become rusted, especially if left in environments that are damp or wet.
- Plastic: Combs made from plastic are the cheapest option since plastic doesn't cost as much to create. Plastic combs give the instrument a less dynamic sound, but can still

work well for any style of music. Many harmonica players say plastic combs feel more comfortable, and they are easier to maintain. The biggest issue you'll find with plastic combs is that they can get cracked, making it impossible to play the harmonica.

- Wood: Combs made from wood will have a warmer sound than other materials. Unfortunately, wood combs are also the most likely to have problems. They can swell or become warped when they get wet. A harmonica with a comb made from wood that's been sealed won't experience this issue, but they will also be much more expensive.

Cover Plates

The cover plates encase the rest of the harmonica and keep the pieces together. They protect the parts inside from damage and environmental effects. The type of cover plates can also affect the overall tone and sound of the harmonica. Picking the right cover plates is a matter of preference, and you need to consider if you'd rather have a cheaper price or a better sound. As a beginner, it might be wiser to buy something of decent quality that's not too expensive, since you can always upgrade your instrument later. The two main types of cover plates include:

- Open Cover Design: This kind of cover plate is composed of plastic or stamped metal. It's made by taking a flat sheet of metal or plastic and using a machine to shape it. The cover plates are secured in place by screws or nails, and because of their simplicity, harmonicas with an open cover design are on the cheaper side. These cover plates aren't meant for much else besides serving as a place to hold the instrument with your hands.

- Closed Cover Design: This type of cover plate encloses the reed plates and comb. It can also have vents, giving the harmonica a louder, richer sound. Chromatic harmonicas usually have a closed cover design, as well as a button or lever on the side to shift the pitch of its notes. Harmonicas with a closed cover design are generally more expensive than those with an open cover design.

Harmonica Equipment and Accessories

In addition to your harmonica, you can make things easier and more convenient for yourself by getting extra gear for your performances, transportation, and storage. You won't need this stuff right away, but it's good to know about what you should think about getting in the future. Once you've gotten better at playing, you can begin adding more equipment and accessories to your stockpile of harmonica gear. Here's a list of some of the gear you might want to buy to go alongside your instrument:

Microphones

There are special microphones designed specifically for harmonicas. They have a large, rounded head, while the back tapers off slightly to a rounded point. It resembles a large bullet, which earned it the nickname "bullet mic." These microphones are easy to hold at the same time as a harmonica, and they will help to boost the sound through any speakers or amplifiers to which the microphone is hooked up. Vocal microphones don't work as well as bullet mics for picking up the sounds of a harmonica but leaving any unwanted noise silenced. If you become serious about performing with your harmonica, a bullet mic is a great investment.

Amplifiers

In order to increase the volume and range of your harmonica's sound, you might want to get an amplifier. They are used together with a microphone to help your playing be heard over the noise of a venue or other musicians while you're performing. Many harmonica players prefer to use tube amplifiers, since for a long time, they offered a much richer, warmer tone. However, solid-state amplifiers have come far with the growth of new technology, and there are some that can copy the sound of tube amplifiers very closely. Guitar amplifiers often double as harmonica amplifiers, and you can get small ones that are easy to carry around, or larger half-stack or full-stack amplifiers when playing shows in big venues.

Neck Racks

A harmonica neck rack is a device that holds your harmonica near your mouth so you can play it without using your hands. This is incredibly useful if you need your hands to do something else, like playing a guitar or piano at the same time. The neck rack has two metal brackets connected to a curved metal loop that sits on your shoulders and is secured behind the neck. A pair of clamps hold your harmonica close to your mouth, keeping it steady and within reach for when you want to start playing it. They're often used by country and folk musicians, like Bob Dylan, who famously played guitar and harmonica himself in many of his songs.

Trays and Stands

Harmonica trays and stands are useful when you have started to collect more harmonicas for different purposes. You can lay out your harmonica collection on the tray and have it attached to a stand so that they're always within reach whenever you play. If you prefer using diatonic harmonicas, you might have a collection where they're all tuned to various keys. Anytime you want to play a song in a specific key, you can swap them out quickly by grabbing a different harmonica right from the stand. It's also a good way to store your harmonicas when you're not playing, since it doesn't take up much room, but is easily accessible whenever you need your harmonicas.

Lip Balm

Since the harmonica is an instrument played with your mouth, there's a good chance your lips are going to suffer some strain. Chapped lips aren't just uncomfortable, but they can make it harder to play. You can find lip balm made specifically for harmonica players. It can be a little more expensive than the kind of stuff you'll find in a drug store, but it's worth spending the extra cash to make sure you won't have to take a break from playing because of damaged lips.

How to Hold Your Harmonica

The proper hand positions when playing your harmonica are important to make sure you get the best sound possible. There are some variations depending on the style of music you're playing, but most beginners start with a basic diatonic harmonica grip. It can take some practice to get right, so don't get upset if you have trouble with it at first. You want to get a good sound while playing, but you should also feel comfortable. Once you've gotten used to holding your harmonica properly, you can begin to experiment with different grips to alter your sound and playing style.

Proper Hand Grip

Finding the right grip starts with something simple. The most popular hand grip involves cupping your hands around your instrument. Here's a step-by-step guide for getting the correct grip while playing your harmonica:

1. Using the thumb and index finger of your left hand, grasp the left side of your harmonica with a pinching motion. Make sure the lowest note is on the left side by blowing into both ends of the mouthpiece.
2. Lay your index finger and thumb flat across the cover plates. Push the harmonica as far toward the space between your thumb and index finger.
3. Shift your harmonica so you're holding it as close to the back as possible. The mouthpiece shouldn't be covered by your fingers or hands.
4. Take your right hand and cup it around your left hand. This will create an air seal around the back of your harmonica. Don't touch the back of the instrument itself—leave a small pocket between your palms and the back of the harmonica.
5. Rest your right thumb along the right side of your harmonica. You will have more control of it while playing using this hand position.
6. Playing the harmonica with your hands cupped will produce a muted tone. If you want a brighter tone, just lift your middle fingers, ring fingers, and pinkies, leaving the rest of the grip the same.
7. Slide your harmonica left or right while keeping your grip the same in order to play each note. Moving your instrument to the right will play higher notes, and moving it to the left will play lower notes.

Posture

The main posture for playing the harmonica is pretty simple, including ways you can position your body to help play comfortably and for many hours. Here's some tips on what you can do with your posture to improve your harmonica playing:

Basic Stance

1. Whether sitting or standing, make sure to keep your back straight. Your neck should be straight as well, and keep your head up while facing directly forward. A straight back and neck makes it easier for air to move in and out of your lungs, which will help you when playing the harmonica.
2. Plant your feet on the floor and keep them shoulder-width apart. This is the best posture for playing, especially if you want to play for a long time. Make sure your feet aren't too close together or too far apart. If they are, it can cause you to hurt yourself and strain your muscles.
3. Relax your shoulders, letting them drop down naturally. Try not to tense or hold them up. Keeping your shoulders relaxed will avoid hurting your neck while playing the harmonica over long periods.
4. Pull your right elbow in so it's pressed against your side. This not only keeps your from hurting yourself, but it also lets you have more control over your harmonica while playing.

Chapter 3: Basic Harmonica Playing Techniques

As you kick off your journey to become a harmonica player, there are some basic techniques you can employ to get you started. These are meant for beginners, so while you will need to practice them to get the hang of the techniques, nothing here should be too hard for you to grasp. Just remember that playing the harmonica is meant to be a fun activity. Many people don't get it right the first time, so don't get discouraged if you need to try it more than once before you figure out how to do these techniques correctly.

There are many techniques to playing the harmonica

Source: https://www.pexels.com/photo/woman-playing-the-harmonica-5967530/

Basic Harmonica Lip Placement

The basic idea for playing the harmonica is to blow air out or suck air in while your mouth is placed over the holes in the comb. The placement of your lips and whether you're blowing or drawing breath will change how the harmonica sounds when played. Interestingly, it's actually easier to play 2 or 3 notes at a time than it is to play a single note. In order to do that, you first need to learn the best ways to put your lips on the mouthpiece when playing.

The Pucker

"The Pucker" is the most basic lip placement for playing the harmonica. The biggest thing to remember is that you don't want to purse your lips with this technique. There shouldn't be much tension in your mouth or jaw when doing the Pucker. When using this technique, you will be able to play single draw or blow notes at a time, isolating them from the surrounding notes. Follow these instructions to get the proper lip placement to play your harmonica:

1. Place your lips on your harmonica in a relaxed position.
2. Tilt your harmonica so the mouthpiece moves down and the back moves up. It should be at about a 30° angle.
3. The top of the mouthpiece will be set deep into your upper lip and on the edge of your bottom lip when done right.
4. Unfold your bottom lip and let the bottom of the mouthpiece rest on the inner portion of the lip. You can use your finger to help you do this if necessary.
5. Draw the corners of your mouth inward, but try to keep your top lip relaxed while puckering your bottom lip. This can take some practice, so try it out a few times until you get the hang of it.
6. Give playing your harmonica a try. If you've done the Pucker correctly, you should only hear a single note being played.

Lip Blocking

Lip blocking can help you play single notes if you're having trouble with the Pucker technique:

1. Follow the instructions for the Pucker lip placement, but once you reach Step 5, rotate your harmonica so the back is pointed completely upward, and the mouthpiece is completely downward.

2. If you try to blow on your harmonica, no sound should come out, since your bottom lip is blocking all the holes.
3. As you're blowing on it, slowly rotate your instrument to bring the mouthpiece up and the back down.
4. Whenever you hear a single note play clearly, stop rotating. You can play your harmonica from this position while you get used to how your lip placement feels.
5. After you've gotten better at playing a single note, you'll be able to rotate your harmonica back into the natural position as described in the Pucker instructions.

Tongue Blocking

Tongue blocking is a more advanced technique for playing 3 notes:

1. Start off by relaxing your lips and widening your mouth across your harmonica's mouthpiece. It should be covering 4 holes of the comb at the same time.
2. Your lips should be slightly pursed, but not as narrow as with the Pucker.
3. Move your tongue forward and to the left in order to cover the lowest note. It should cover the leftmost hole within the span of your mouth.
4. Fold your tongue as much as possible to avoid blocking the higher 3 notes.
5. When you play the 3 uncovered notes, you will be using the right side of your mouth to blow or draw breath. Try to aim for playing the highest note in the group.

6. Make sure the notes you're playing sound clean. There shouldn't be any sign of the lowest note covered by your tongue leaking through.
7. If you can't get this technique right, don't worry— only about 50% of people in the world are able to fold their tongue completely. Even if you can only fold it slightly, with practice, you might be able to get tongue blocking to work.

Breath Control

Breath control is important to playing the harmonica since your breath is the main thing creating the instrument's sound. Unlike something like a saxophone, tuba, trumpet, flute, or trombone, there aren't any keys, holes, or slides that help to play the right notes alongside your breath. This makes it incredibly important to have control of your breathing when you play your harmonica.

Belly Breathing Technique

Part of playing the harmonica is using the proper breathing technique. This will let the notes you play come out strong and last as long as you need. You don't want your harmonica to sound weak or airy, which will happen if you don't breathe correctly while playing. The right kind of breathing doesn't come from your chest but from your diaphragm. To learn the proper belly breathing technique, follow these instructions:

1. Lay down flat on your back.
2. Place your left hand on your chest and your right hand on your belly.
3. Breathe in deeply, using your diaphragm, which is located near your belly. When done right, you

should feel your right hand move up, while your left hand on your chest remains still.

4. Let your breath out, again feeling your right hand lower down and keeping your left hand still.

5. Repeat breathing in and out. Picture yourself filling a balloon in your belly with air. Nothing else should be moving when you fill it up, and nothing else should move when you let the air out again.

6. Breathe in and out this way 20 times (20 times in and 20 times out). Practice this regularly, until it becomes automatic. Use this type of breathing when playing the harmonica.

Breath Control Exercise

Practicing your breath control will let you be able to blow and draw notes over long periods of time. This is essential if you're going to be playing music, especially songs that involve the harmonica throughout the entire composition. To do this exercise, follow these steps:

1. Place your lips on the mouthpiece and keep them relaxed. It doesn't matter where on the harmonica you place them.

2. Let your shoulders fall down and keep your throat relaxed. Your tongue should be resting in your mouth gently and not interfering with your playing.

3. Breathe in and out, but don't change the shape of your mouth. You should be able to cover 3 holes with your mouth when it's relaxed.

4. Continue to breathe in and out repeatedly. Keep your breathing even. When drawing and blowing, the sound that comes out of your harmonica will be different.

5. Don't worry if the sound your harmonica makes is a bit sloppy. Right now, focus solely on your breathing. Keep inhaling and exhaling with even breaths.

6. Make sure the amount of air you're blowing is equal to the amount of air you're taking in. The air should be moving easily into your lungs and back out again. Use the speed and volume of the sound your harmonica makes to help you keep your breathing steady. If done right, you shouldn't be running out of breath, allowing you to play for a long time.

Yawning Exercise

Yawning can help you to learn how to relax your throat properly. It forces you to open your mouth wide and lets oxygen move freely to your lungs. When your throat is relaxed and open with air flowing through it easily, it's known as the "fat pipe." You can use the fat pipe to breathe air in and out gently without anything getting in its way. Moving air in and out of your lungs through an open and relaxed throat should happen silently. If your breathing is making any noise, open your throat again by yawning and hold it in that position without tensing up. This should allow the air to move back and forth without any noise again.

After you've gotten used to how your throat feels while yawning, you can practice doing it without opening your mouth wide. Instead, while yawning, do the Pucker with your lips. Try it a few times to get used to the feeling. While keeping your throat open and your lips in the correct placement, add in your harmonica. Breathe in and out like you were before, letting the air move gently through your lungs. The waves of sound created by playing the harmonica will move through your airway and come out strong. This is the way your throat should always be when performing. If you feel your throat closing up or becoming tense, take your harmonica away and yawn again to relax it again.

Nose Blocking

When playing your harmonica, any air that's not being used to directly play notes is considered leakage. It makes the sound weaker and can make it harder to play for long periods of time. The obvious source of leakage is air passing through extra holes in the comb when you don't want that to happen. Another major source of leakage is air escaping through your nose while playing. You might not be used to stopping the airflow through your nose without holding it closed with your fingers, so you need to practice doing this without actually touching your nose. The best nose-blocking exercise is also known as the "balloon exercise." You can do this exercise by following these steps:

1. Purse your lips and touch them to the back of your hand. Your mouth should be in the same shape you'd make when blowing up a balloon.
2. Using the muscles in the back of your throat and the sides of your nose, try to "plug" it up. Think about what you do when going underwater. The soft area in the back of your throat moves up and the muscles beside your nose move inward.
3. When you try to blow air out if your nose is plugged, the air won't have anywhere else to go. It will make your cheeks puff out as you exhale.
4. Try to inhale. If your nose remains plugged, it will make your cheeks suck in.
5. You will know you can plug your nose to block the airflow and prevent leakage if done correctly. Keep

practicing it if you don't get the hang of it right away.

6. After you've completed the balloon exercise, use the same technique of plugging your nose when playing the harmonica to prevent leakage.

Blowing and Drawing Techniques

Blowing notes are the notes you play while exhaling and draw notes are the ones played while inhaling. On most harmonicas, they will sound different and play a different note on the same hole. Making these notes sound clean and come out correctly can take practice, and there are some techniques and exercises you can use to be sure you're doing it right. Even the top professional harmonica players had to start somewhere. At one point in their lives, they were doing the same thing as you. Keep that in mind as motivation as you learn how to blow and draw notes.

Playing Blow Notes

Blow notes are played when you're breathing air out of your lungs and through your mouth. To do it the right way, follow these directions:

1. Get into the proper posture for playing the harmonica.
2. Relax your throat and let your shoulders fall.
3. Using the Pucker, place your mouth on your harmonica.
4. Choose which note you wish to play and position your lips over the correct hole.
5. Breathe in through your nose and fill your lungs with air.

6. Plug your nose and exhale with a gentle, even breath. This will cause the note you chose to play.

Playing Draw Notes

Draw notes are played when you're breathing air into your lungs through your mouth. As with blow notes, you can follow these instructions to play them:

1. Repeat Steps 1 through 4 from the blow note directions.
2. With your lips in position over the correct hole for the note you want to play, inhale with a gentle, even breath.
3. You will hear your chosen note play. Remember that it will be a different note than the blow note played on the same hole.

Blow and Draw Note Endurance

When playing blow and draw notes, you don't want to huff air out or suck it in too hard. Using the proper breathing techniques and lip placement, practice playing by breathing in and out gently:

1. Start off by placing your lips on the lowest hole in the comb, all the way to the left. Test out that your lip placement is correct and you're only playing a single note.
2. Breathe in deeply, letting the draw note go on for 5 to 10 seconds.
3. Then breathe out in the same way, letting the blow note also last for 5 to 10 seconds.
4. Change to the next hole to the right and repeat Steps 2 and 3.

5. After repeating Steps 2 and 3, continue doing the same thing with each hole to the right until you reach the highest note.
6. Once you play the highest note, move back to the next hole to the left and repeat Steps 2 and 3.
7. Continue back down the notes of the harmonica until you reach the beginning again.
8. Practice this for about 5 minutes.
9. The next time you practice your endurance, add another 5 minutes.
10. Keep adding an additional 5 minutes until you've gotten used to playing with the right blowing and drawing technique without needing to stop.

Getting a Sense of Pitch and Tone

You can view pitch and tone as two sides of the same coin. They are both parts of how your harmonica sounds when you play it. Pitch describes how high or low the notes you play are, while tone is the strength of the sound and its overall quality. When playing the harmonica, you control the pitch based on which notes you play and where they are along the comb. It's also affected by whether you're playing blow or draw notes on a certain hole. If you use bending techniques, you can raise or drop the pitch down by a half step, whole step, or a step and a half to add more notes into the mix.

The tone of your harmonica is controlled by your breathing techniques. How hard you blow or draw air in and out of your lungs while playing is going to change the tone. Playing softly will give the tone an airy quality, while playing harder makes the tone stronger and stand out more. Depending on the type of mood you want to give off to the listener, you can change the tone of your harmonica's sound. Sadder songs or parts of a song are better when you play with a softer tone. This gives off a darker mood while playing. Exciting songs or musical pieces work best when they are played with a strong, bright tone.

Chapter 4: Learning to Play the Harmonica

After you've become good enough at playing basic notes on their own, you can start putting a string of notes together to play actual music. It's going to take plenty of practice before you sound like a true harmonica player, but it's worth the effort. The harmonica is a great instrument to play on its own or as an accompaniment to a larger musical group. When you can play songs cleanly and without mistakes, you can start performing for audiences. The ultimate goal of any harmonica player is to get out in front of a crowd and wow them with your skills.

How to Bend Notes

Bending notes is a special technique you can use to shift the pitch of regular notes on the harmonica to go up or down between half a step and a step and a half. This opens up the amount of notes you can play on a typical harmonica, especially a diatonic harmonica. It's often necessary to bend notes in order to have access to the full range of notes in a chromatic scale. There are 12 notes in a scale, but many harmonicas can only play 7 of those notes with basic blow and draw notes. Bending the blow and draw notes lets you play the missing 5 notes on the scale so you can use the entire thing.

For example, the chromatic scale for G includes the notes: G, G♯, A, A♯, B, C, C♯, D, D♯, E, E♯, and F♯. However, a G major diatonic harmonica will only be able to play G, A, B, C, D, E, and F♯ without the use of blow notes. Adding the notes reached by using bends, a diatonic harmonica tuned to G major will look like this:

	1	2	3	4	5	6	7	8	9	10
1 Step										F
½ Step								A♯	C♯	F♯
Blow	G	B	D	G	B	D	G	B	D	G
Draw	A	D	F♯	A	C	E	F♯	A	C	E
½ Step	G♯	C♯	F	G♯		D♯				
1 Step		C	E							

1 ½ Step			D♯							

Bending blow and draw notes involves moving the position of your tongue in your mouth while breathing in or out. Where your tongue is placed will change the way the air flows from your mouth and into the harmonica. The airflow will either be "bent" upward or downward, changing the way it enters the holes of the comb and affecting the pitch that comes out. To understand this effect, try whistling. Move your tongue up and down in your mouth while you're whistling. You'll notice that it makes your whistling sound higher or lower, depending on which way you move your tongue. Bending notes on the harmonica works just like that, except the sound is coming from the instrument instead of your lips.

Bending Blow Notes

The blow notes you can bend are in holes 8, 9, and 10. These notes will bend a half step or whole step up from the regular blow notes. In order to bend blow notes, you need to follow these steps:

1. Start off using the Pucker, just like you would when playing a single note.
2. Lift your tongue toward the roof of your mouth. It can sometimes help if you pull your jaw inward while doing this to get the right positioning.
3. Tighten your throat until it's almost closed up. You want to narrow the passageway through which the air flows to help bend the note.

4. Exhale and listen to the note being played. Adjust your tongue to get the correct pitch. It will be a half step above the original blow note.
5. Avoid blowing harder than normal while breathing out to play. Everything you need to do to bend a blow note happens with your tongue and throat. The rest is played just like any other note.

Bending Draw Notes

The draw notes you can bend are in holes 1, 2, 3, 4, and 6. Like with blow notes, bending is mainly controlled by your tongue and throat. To bend draw notes, follow these instructions:

1. Start off using the Pucker, as if you're playing regular single draw notes.
2. Drop your tongue down toward the base of your mouth. You can push your jaw outward to help position it correctly.
3. Expand your throat as wide as possible. You want there to be a maximum amount of airflow coming through it.
4. Inhale and listen to the pitch of the note being played. It should be a half step below the original draw note. Make any necessary adjustments to reach the right bent draw note.
5. Don't suck in air too hard. You should still be playing the bent draw note the same as you would any regular draw note.

Bending Notes Higher and Lower Than a Half-Step

If you want to bend the blow and draw notes higher or lower than a half step, you have that option on a few holes. You can bend the draw notes on holes 2 and 3 a whole step down, and a step and a half on hole 3. You can also bend the blow note on hole 10 up a whole step. To reach the lower draw notes, you have to drop your tongue down lower and control the airflow from your throat. Going in the opposite direction, bending the blow notes higher is achieved by lifting your tongue higher and tightening your throat even more. It will take a lot of practice to reach the whole step and step-and-a-half bend notes. Chances are you won't get it right away. Trial and error is the best way to figure out exactly how to position your tongue when you hear the right notes played from your harmonica.

Understanding Harmonica Sheet Music

Harmonica sheet music is different from regular sheet music. Instead of having notes placed along a treble or bass clef, harmonica sheet music shows you which numbered hole you need to play, and whether you need to play it as a blow or draw note. It will also usually give you a basic count for the beat of the music. On beats that you don't play anything, the space will be left blank. Here's an example of some basic harmonica sheet music:

Count	1 2 3 4	1 2 3 4	1 2 3 4	1 2 3 4
Blow	11	333	5	55 5
Draw	22	4	444	

Blow	6 7	88	10	6 32
Draw	7 7	9	10 8	4

Practicing Simple Melodies

Putting together all the skills you've learned, you can take a shot at playing some simple melodies on the harmonica. Here are 3 easy songs you can start with to get used to playing basic melodies. The graphs below show you which numbered holes to play and whether they should be a blow or draw note.

Mary Had a Little Lamb

Count	1 2 3 4	1 2 3 4	1 2 3 4	1 2 3 4
Blow	5 4	5 5 5		5 5 5
Draw	4 4		4 4 4	

Blow	5 4	5 5 5 4	5	4
Draw	4 4		4 4 4	

This Old Man

Count	1 2 3 4	1 2 3 4	1 2 3 4	1 2 3 4
Blow	6 5 6	6 5 6	6 5	5 5
Draw			6 5	4 5 5

Blow	6 4 4 4 4	4 5 6	6	5 4
Draw		4 5	4 4 5	4

Twinkle, Twinkle Little Star

Count	1 2 3 4	1 2 3 4	1 2 3 4	1 2 3 4
Blow	4 4 6 6	6	5 5	4
Draw		6 6	5 5	4 4
Blow	4 4 6 6	6	5 5	4
Draw		6 6	5 5	4 4
Blow	6 6	5 5	6 6	5 5
Draw	5 5	4	5 5	4
Blow	4 4 6 6	6	5 5	4
Draw		6 6	5 5	4 4

Creating a Good Practice Routine

Dedicating yourself to practicing the harmonica is the only way to get better at playing. While you can practice whenever you have some free time, it can help to create a regular practice routine. This kind of structure will make it easier to be sure you don't slack off with how often or how hard you practice. You want to always push yourself to improve, so your routine needs to evolve over time. Each time you practice, you should aim to do something that's a bit more difficult than what you did during the last practice session. Here's an example of a basic practice routine you can use:

1. Start by going up the harmonica from the lowest note to the highest, playing all blow notes in holes 1 through 10.
2. Go back down the harmonica from the highest note to the lowest, playing all blow notes in holes 10 through 1.

3. Repeat Step 1 and 2, but this time play all draw notes.
4. Go up the harmonica and alternate between blow notes and draw notes. Start with a blow note on hole 1, then a draw note on hole 2, a blow note on hole 3, a draw note on hole 4, and keep going like that up to hole 10.
5. Go down the harmonica again, but this time reverse which holes are blow notes and which are draw notes. Start with a blow note on hole 10, then a draw note on hole 9, a blow note on hole 8, a draw note on hole 7, and keep going in that order down to hole 1.
6. Next, you can try practicing bending the blow and draw notes. See if you can bend the blow notes on holes 8, 9, and 10 up a half step.
7. After you've practiced bending blow notes, do the same thing with draw notes. Try to bend the draw notes on holes 1, 2, 3, 4, and 6 down a half step.
8. When you feel like you've had a good warmup and feel comfortable with playing single notes, give it a shot playing one of the simple melodies you've learned. Go through the entire song several times until you've gotten it down without making any mistakes. Your notes should sound strong and clear.

The next time you practice, add in a more complicated routine during the warmups, like skipping every other hole while alternating between blow and draw notes. You can also find longer and harder songs to play. Don't be afraid to really test your abilities. Even if you have trouble getting it right, just focus on one section of the song. The next time you practice, you can focus on the next section until you can play it correctly. Eventually, you'll be able to play the entire song without a problem.

Chapter 5: Becoming a Better Harmonica Player

In order to become an expert harmonica player, you need to find ways to sharpen your skills. Knowing the basics of playing the harmonica can only get you so far. If you're looking to tackle more complicated songs and musical compositions, you have to work hard and keep improving your abilities. The best harmonica players are dedicated to their craft, and they tell you that you never stop learning how to get better, no matter how skilled you are at the moment.

Tips and Tricks during Practice

Here are some tips and tricks you can use while practicing to help you improve your skills as a harmonica player:

- Don't Get Down on Yourself: There will be points when you can't seem to get things right. You might start questioning if you'll ever be able to play well enough. The trick is to ignore that voice in your head telling you, "I can't do this." Instead, tell yourself, "I can do this, and I will do it."

- Give Yourself a Minimum Amount of Practice Time: It takes a certain amount of time and effort to become good at anything. Only practicing a few minutes here and there isn't going to cut it. You should be practicing for a minimum of at least 10 minutes per session. If you really want to improve your harmonica playing skills, aim for 15 to 30 minutes as a minimum amount of practice time per session.
- Make It a Point to Practice Every Day: The amount of time you practice during a session isn't going to do much good if you only practice once a week. Any serious musician knows that you need to be practicing every single day. This kind of repetition is the only way you will hone your skills and improve your playing abilities.
- Play Along with Music: Whether you have a way to play music live or simply use a recording, find a way to play your harmonica along with it. Make sure the songs you're playing along with are in the same key as the harmonica you're using. With live musicians, they can jam by playing a basic chord progression in your chosen key and let you improvise while showing off your skills.
- Take a Break When You Need It: Sometimes you'll hit a wall with a certain technique or song you're trying to learn. It can get frustrating, and if you've been pushing for a while without success, the best thing you can do is take a break. Go do something else for a

while to get your mind off it. When you return to practice again, you'll be refreshed and in a better headspace to get it right.

Harmonica Care and Maintenance

Every type of musician has a responsibility to keep their instrument playing and sounding right. Taking care of your harmonica is an important part of being a harmonica player. There are some tips and tricks you can use to help you make sure your harmonica is always in tip-top shape. It can be boring and tiresome, but it's a part of being a harmonica player. You should perform regular maintenance on your instrument to make sure it's in working order. This doesn't have to be something you do every time you play, but it's a good idea to check over your harmonica once every week or two.

Common Problems

Sometimes screws come loose, dirt or debris can get inside it, or the reeds need replacement. A common issue is spit getting stuck in the holes of the comb. Here are some tricks you can use to help keep your harmonica clean and ready to play:

- Bang your harmonica against the bottom of the palm of your hand a few times. Then breathe in and out hard over the holes of the comb. This should get any saliva out and clear up the sound.
- If there's something stuck in one of the reeds, you can use a toothpick to get the dirt or debris out. Move the reed very gently in and out with one end of the toothpick, then turn your

harmonica over and tap it to make sure everything comes out.

- Use a small screwdriver (like one from a harmonica service set or a glasses repair kit) to remove the cover plates. Check the reeds for anything stuck in them that's larger than some tiny pieces of dirt or debris. Sometimes this is a hair or larger chunk of dirt that got into your instrument.

Service Sets

Service sets are specialized maintenance kits that contain everything you need to make sure your harmonica is in working order. Most service sets will include the following tools:

- Tuning scraper
- Reed lifting blade
- Reed wrench
- Fine-tuning file
- Hook tool
- Slot screwdriver
- Phillips screwdriver
- Valve glue
- Set of valves
- Cleaning cloth

Storage and Handling Guidelines

To keep your harmonicas safe, you should get storage cases for them. You can buy individual cases, such as pouch cases, which hold only a single harmonica. There are also larger cases meant to hold a collection of harmonicas. These cases are usually hard cover cases, which offer more protection for your instruments. If your harmonicas are made of any materials that can warp, rust, or crack when exposed to certain environmental effects, having a case is the best way to prevent them from becoming damaged. You can safely store your harmonicas in a closet or basement without worrying about what might happen to them if the storage space is a bit too damp or overly dry.

Chapter 6: Exploring Harmonica History and Repertoire

The harmonica hasn't been around as long as many other instruments, but that doesn't mean its history is boring. If you need evidence for this, just look at some of the most famous harmonica players and how they used the harmonica to record hit songs that have withstood the test of time. For such a little thing, the harmonica has a pretty big story behind it.

History of the Harmonica

The early 19th century saw the invention of the harmonica as we know it today. The person given credit for inventing the harmonica is a man named Christian Friedrich Ludwig Buschmann. It's believed he first introduced his new instrument in 1821. Interestingly, he is also said to be the inventor of the accordion, another free-reed wind instrument. Charles Wheatstone started selling the Aeolina, a musical instrument similar to the harmonica, in 1829. They were mostly utilized in classical music performed in Europe, South America, and the United States.

After harmonicas began being sold in Vienna, Austria, Joseph Richter invented "Richter tuning," a way of tuning the instrument that was adopted by harmonica makers across the world. It became the standard tuning method from 1826 and is still used in diatonic harmonicas to this day. In 1857, a German clockmaker named Matthias Hohner became the first person to mass-produce harmonicas. He started selling his version of the instrument with a machine-cut wooden comb to the United States in 1868, spreading its popularity because it was cheap and easy to make.

By the 20th century, harmonicas were a common sight in five and dimes, hobby shops, and music stores. Blues and jazz musicians began incorporating the instrument into their music during the early part of the century. Harmonicas were perfect for improvisation since many were tuned to a specific key, meaning they couldn't really play it off-key while accompanying other musicians performing in the same key. As the technology of harmonicas improved, the things artists could do with them expanded greatly. The 1960s saw the rise of folk rock, and there were many famous musicians who used harmonicas on their hit songs. Rock music with a bluesy style also had harmonicas as a common feature.

From the 1960s to the 1980s, the harmonica appeared in plenty of popular music. However, as electronic music, hard rock, and rap became more prominent throughout the 1980s, the harmonica faded from the forefront of popular culture. The use of electronic keyboards and digital synthesizers also reduced the need for harmonicas and other wind instruments, since their sounds could all be easily reproduced by a single musician. From that point on, right up to the modern day, music with real harmonicas being played are reserved for niche genres and underground musical cultures.

Cultural Impact of the Harmonica

During the American Civil War, harmonicas became a source of comfort for soldiers on both the Union and Confederate sides. President Abraham Lincoln even carried one and liked to play it during quiet moments when he wanted to distract himself from the problems facing the country. The famous Wild West lawman Wyatt Earp and outlaw cowboy Billy the Kid were both known for their harmonica playing skills, popularizing the instrument as a staple of the period. It's now rare to see a movie about the Wild West where somebody doesn't pull out a harmonica and start blowing on it.

The connection between harmonicas and soldiers continued in World War II. They became rare for civilians in the United States, mainly because the materials were being used to help out with the war effort, and many of the overseas makers were located in Germany and Japan—two of the Allies' biggest enemies at the time. However, the War Department made sure the largest harmonica producer in the United States still had enough materials to make them for the soldiers, and they were given out alongside food, cigarettes, and other supplies to help with morale.

In the mid-20th century, the process of creating harmonicas was made cheaper by the introduction of molded plastic materials. Because the harmonica could be bought with very little money and wasn't too complicated to use, it became common to give to children. The first instrument many kids got was a harmonica. Since most people had owned, at least tried blowing into one, there was no shortage of the instrument being on sale at shops around the globe. The chances of someone reaching the age of 18 without ever seeing a harmonica is very low. This kind of widespread awareness is something very few things in modern culture can claim.

Famous Harmonica Players

The best harmonica players are usually known for more than just their harmonica playing. While the harmonica is a wonderful instrument with a great sound, it's rare for it to "carry" a song. Those most famous for playing the harmonica also tend to be lead singers, and sometimes guitarists as well. It's a skill that's certainly highly-valued, but if you want to have a career as a professional musician, you will need to do more than become great at playing the harmonica. You can follow in the footsteps of the best harmonica players who came before you, working hard to master the instrument alongside whatever else you have a talent for doing.

Little Walter

Marion Walter Jacobs, known professionally as "Little Walter," was a blues musician in the 1940s and 1950s who redefined the harmonica for generations to come. Called the "Jimi Hendrix of the Blues Harmonica," his skills pushed what people viewed as possible with the instrument beyond anything that had come before him. He was inducted into the Rock and Roll Hall of Fame in 2008 and remains the only musician in the Hall of Fame specifically as a harmonica player.

John Popper

John Popper is the lead singer and harmonica player for the rock band Blues Traveler. He is considered a virtuoso with the harmonica, adding a rapid-fire, complex sound to his music. Two standout tracks include "Run-Around" and "Hook" from the band's 1994 album four. Due to his abilities, his harmonica playing has been featured on dozens of tracks by other artists. He is the go-to harmonica player whenever a major recording artist wants a great sounding harmonica in the mix of their music.

Big Mama Thornton

Willie Mae Thornton, known to audiences as "Big Mama Thornton," was a blues and R&B artist who became famous during the middle of the 20th century for her booming voice, bombastic stage presence, and harmonica playing. She was the first artist to record the song "Hound Dog," later popularized by Elvis Presley. Another song, "Ball and Chain," became a hit for Janis Joplin in the 1960s. Many of Thornton's songs were re-recorded by later artists, but due to the way royalties worked back then, she never saw a dime. However, she will always be remembered for the influence she had on later musicians, as well as her skilled harmonica playing.

Bob Dylan

Robert Allen Zimmerman, better known as "Bob Dylan," became famous for his work as a singer-songwriter in the 1960s. He wrote poetic folk music that often featured harmonica playing as a core element. His songs "Like a Rolling Stone" and "The Times They Are a-Changin'" were used as anthems for the rebellious and discontented 1960s youth, especially in their protests over things like Civil Rights and the Vietnam War. Dylan's connection to the harmonica is so iconic that you will rarely see a picture of him playing music without a harmonica hooked up to his neck rack in addition to the acoustic guitar in his hands.

John Lennon

John Lennon was a singer, songwriter, and multi-instrumentalist who skyrocketed to fame as a member of the Beatles. During his time with the iconic "Fab Four," Lennon contributed his harmonica playing skills on many different songs, including, "Love Me Do," "Rocky Raccoon," "I'll Get You," "Little Child," "From Me To You," "There's A Place," and "Thank You Girl." He learned to play the instrument on a toy harmonica as a child, mainly teaching himself. When a bus driver heard how good Lennon was, he gave the boy a professional harmonica from the lost and found box on the bus. Lennon continued to practice, and by the time he formed the Beatles with Paul McCartney, George Harrison, Stuart Sutcliffe, and Pete Best (Sutcliffe left the band for health reasons and McCartney switched from guitar to bass; Best was fired and replaced on drums by Ringo Starr), he was good enough to perform on the band's recordings.

Important Harmonica Compositions

Some of the most important compositions for the harmonica were produced between the 1960s and early 1980s. It was during this period that the harmonica-playing singer-songwriter boom reached the peak of its popularity. Folk-rock and blues-inspired rock and roll entered the mainstream, giving songs featuring the harmonica a high amount of visibility. While the musical landscape shifted significantly in the 1980s and the decades that followed, these songs continue to hold a special place in the history of music.

"Heart of Gold" by Neil Young

"Heart of Gold" was released by Neil Young on his 1972 album Harvest. The track was written after Young suffered a back injury that made it difficult for him to stand. As a result, he swapped his electric guitar for an acoustic while composing the song, and added in the harmonica parts as the only other instrument he could easily play and perform with while still in too much pain to stand or move around. The iconic harmonica melody starts off right away during the song's intro, and returns during each of the instrument-only breaks throughout the track.

"Piano Man" by Billy Joel

"Piano Man" was released as the titular track by Billy Joel on his 1973 album of the same name. It has become iconic as a standard for singing along to at parties and bars whenever it plays. The lyrics reflect Joel's experiences when playing the piano as a lounge musician in Los Angeles while he was trying to make a name for himself. His rousing chorus solidified the track as a signature song when playing live. The harmonica melody is just as notable as the rest of the song, and Joel performed them himself on the original recording.

"Roadhouse Blues" by The Doors

"Roadhouse Blues" was released by rock band The Doors on their 1970 album Morrison Hotel. It's one of the band's most popular songs, having been covered by many other artists over the years. According to Bruce Botnick, the sound engineer for the track, "Roadhouse Blues" is the "all-time American bar band song." John Sebastian, the former front man of the seminal 1960s folk-rock band The Lovin' Spoonful, provided the harmonica parts for the track. In both his own music and on "Roadhouse Blues," Sebastian's talented performance shows just how much mileage you can get from an instrument like the harmonica.

"The Jean Genie" by David Bowie

David Bowie

Source: AVRO, CC BY-SA 3.0 NL
<https://creativecommons.org/licenses/by-sa/3.0/nl/deed.en>, via
Wikimedia Commons:
https://commons.wikimedia.org/wiki/File:David_Bowie_-
_TopPop_1974_03_(cropped).png

"The Jean Genie" was released by David Bowie on his 1973 album Aladdin Sane. The song began as an improvised tune played during a jam session undertaken by the band in between concerts on the Ziggy Stardust Tour. Bowie later took the riffs from the jam session and wrote the song as the first one composed for his new album. While writing "The Jean Genie," Bowie decided to add harmonica parts to the track, which he played himself during the recording sessions. It's a very, blues-inspired melody that sounds like the sort of thing you'd hear on songs from the 1930s and 1940s.

"Mr. Tambourine Man" by Bob Dylan

"Mr. Tambourine Man" was released by Bob Dylan on his 1965 album Bringing It All Back Home. The album is notable for being split into two halves: the first 7 songs were recorded with Dylan playing electric guitar, a new and controversial choice for the artist, while the last 4 songs used Dylan's traditional acoustic arrangements. "Mr. Tambourine Man" was the first of the acoustic songs, and featured his signature harmonica playing in an iconic solo during the bridge and outro. His harmonica playing helps to ground the lyrics, which are widely considered to be a poetic tribute to illegal drugs.

"The River" by Bruce Springsteen

"The River" was released as the titular track by Bruce Springsteen on his 1980 double album of the same name. It was inspired by his sister and brother-in-law and features the E Street Band on the track as his backing musicians. The harmonica melody featured helps give the song a feeling of haunting nostalgia, serving as a fitting companion to lyrics filled with melancholic memories and long-held regrets. Springsteen played the harmonica parts himself on the track, and later used these skills more in his future music, especially his 1982 album Nebraska.

Conclusion

This book has given you what you need to become a better harmonica player. You know every part of your harmonica and what each one does. You understand the basics of how to play and read harmonica sheet music. All the tips, tricks, techniques, and exercises are there to help you advance to the next level. Whenever you need to go back and review the material, just check any section you want and read up on the great information in this guide.

Having the ability to play a musical instrument will open up many doors for you. If you know other musicians, you can now join them whenever they get together to play. It can also be a springboard for you to learn other instruments, or even work on your vocal skills. A harmonica is great on its own, but it's even better when you can play it alongside something else. Just like the most famous harmonica players, being able to add the harmonica to instruments like a guitar, piano, or singing will spruce up a song and turn it from a run-of-the-mill performance to a memorable hit.

Learning to play the harmonica is just like learning any other skill—you have to be dedicated to getting better if you want to succeed. If you aren't willing to train yourself with the various techniques or practice the fundamentals, you'll be stuck at square one. However, if you put in the time and effort to improve, you'll work your way up from beginner to expert. There's never a better time to take the next step than right now. With everything you've learned from this book, you're more than ready to succeed as a great harmonica player!

References

Allen, J. P. (2010, April 15). How to Buy the Right Harmonica –
What Really Matters. Harmonica.com.
https://www.harmonica.com/things-you-need-to-know-
before-buying-harmonica/

Allen, J. P. (2012a, August 21). All About Harmonica Holes and
Notes – Discover the Difference Between Blow + Draw Notes.
Harmonica.com. https://www.harmonica.com/harmonica-
notes-understanding-the-holes-for-playing-songs/

Allen, J. P. (2012b, October 24). Harmonica Breathing
Technique Made Easy. Harmonica.com.
https://www.harmonica.com/harmonica-breathing/

Allen, J. P. (2012c, October 24). How to Hold a Harmonica.
Harmonica.com. https://www.harmonica.com/how-to-hold-a-
harmonica/

Densley, K. (2023, August 25). Almanac Music: John Lennon's
Harmonica. Www.footyalmanac.com.au.
https://www.footyalmanac.com.au/almanac-music-john-
lennons-harmonica/

Farrant, D. (2023, May 12). 15 Famous Harmonica Players you
Should Know | HelloMusicTheory.
Https://Hellomusictheory.com/.

https://hellomusictheory.com/learn/famous-harmonica-players/

Luke. (2019, October 25). How to Play Single Notes on Harmonica – For Beginners. Harmonica.com. https://www.harmonica.com/single-notes/

Luke. (2022, March 22). Exploring the 3 Types of Harmonica – A Beginner's Guide. Harmonica.com. https://www.harmonica.com/exploring-the-3-types-of-harmonica/

The Good Doctor. (2021, May 3). Blow Bends – Harp Surgery. Www.harpsurgery.com. https://www.harpsurgery.com/how-to-play/blow-bends/

themusicstand.ca. (2018a, May 4). Bending Notes With The Harmonica. TheMusicStand.ca. https://www.themusicstand.ca/blogs/htp-harmonica/bending

themusicstand.ca. (2018b, May 5). How To Breathe When Playing Harmonica. TheMusicStand.ca. https://www.themusicstand.ca/blogs/htp-harmonica/breathe

themusicstand.ca. (2018c, May 6). How to Hold Your Harmonica. TheMusicStand.ca. https://www.themusicstand.ca/blogs/htp-harmonica/hold

Ward, L. (2022, November 8). How to Play Harmonica in 15 Steps | Beginner Harmonica Lessons. LearnTheHarmonica. https://www.learntheharmonica.com/post/how-to-play-harmonica-15-steps-beginner

Ward, L. (2023, March 14). Top 10 Most Famous Harmonica Songs. LearnTheHarmonica. https://www.learntheharmonica.com/post/top-10-most-famous-harmonica-songs

wikiHow Staff. (2021, August 10). How to Hold a Harmonica: 10 Steps (with Pictures). WikiHow. https://www.wikihow.com/Hold-a-Harmonica

Yerxa, W. (2023, February 14). Breathing Exercises for Harmonica Players. Dummies. https://www.dummies.com/article/academics-the-arts/music/instruments/harmonica/breathing-exercises-for-harmonica-players-146671/

Made in United States
Troutdale, OR
11/26/2024

25282588R10040